To Touch a Woman

Robert Dollarhide

Order this book online at www.trafford.com
or email orders@trafford.com

Most Trafford titles are also available at major online book retailers.

Printed in the United States of America.

ISBN: 978-1-4269-6748-1 (sc)
ISBN: 978-1-4269-6749-8 (e)

Library of Congress Control Number: 2011906573

Trafford rev. 04/26/2011

 www.trafford.com

North America & international
toll-free: 1 888 232 4444 (USA & Canada)
phone: 250 383 6864 ♦ fax: 812 355 4082

I would like to extend my heartfelt appreciation to Armene for graciously allowing me to use her art for the cover of this book. For more of her art and photography go to http://armene.deviantart.com/ or www.armene. com.

A Beautiful Thing

That first kiss!
Lips, so very, very soft.
So sweet, so lovely.
Holding you in my arms.
Feeling you against me.
Kissing you under the soft light of the moon.
You are such a beautiful thing.
Touching the soft line of your jaw,
Your smooth cheek.
I had wanted to since that night we sat on the couch watching movies.
I spent most of the time watching you.
Soaking in details.
So pretty, such fine features.
The slight pressure and warmth as you leaned against me.
This night we stand embraced.
The sound of waves, the cool breeze, a soft still night.
Moonlight broken by scattered clouds.
The feeling as I touched the small of your back.
The feel of your skin against my hand.
You felt amazing.
The athletic lines of your body.
Under the softness of skin.
Warmth against the coolness of night.
Such perfection of form.
Holding you, swaying to unheard music.
I loved the initial explorations of your body.
You felt so very good.
I am in awe thinking about it as I write this.
Your kisses, the way you felt under my touch.
You took my breath away.
I could feel such a radiance about you.
It stilled me and made my heart skip a beat.
To which you can attest.
So beautiful under the moonlight.
Such a sweet scent.

Such a beautiful thing.
I haven't kissed a woman so much in a long time.
And I enjoyed it above all things.
It was such an incredible feeling.
You drew something out of me that I had forgotten existed.
That version of love without the mask of the world wrapped around it.
A true and honest feeling.
I knew that I would do whatever I could to make you happy.
To make myself worthy of your love.
You are worth my very best.
And so much more.
You are the kind of woman I had dreamed of,
When love first formed in my mind so long ago.
A love that seemed so unreal that I put it out of my mind.
And forgot that it existed.
A love that I forgot that I,
Or anyone else,
Was capable of.
It amazes me that I had forgotten what love really felt like.
I know I must be patient.
I must wait for you and your acceptance.
I will be patient.
You are worth it.
I say to you that I will,
And I mean it with every ounce of my being.
And I say with wonder and surety under the face of God.
That this will be such a beautiful thing.

A Good Woman

I saw you again today.
It has been months.
Withdrawals for me,
burning you out of my system.
And yet talking to you refreshes my soul.
You are a good woman.
Beautiful and so fun to be around.
The kind of woman it is easy to spend hours around.
Not an easy task for me.
I have been impatient with my desires around you,
And with others.
It is different now though.
Not the sexually motivated fervor as before.
We are comforts to each other's hearts.
Tried and true refuges.
We love each other.
But in that truer and better way.
Dear to each other.
Fond memories.
We remember our love and let our mistakes fall by the wayside.
Friends tight.
Not lovers but we love one another.
You my dear sweet girl,
My lovely woman.
You are the best among women.

A Seed of Inspiration

That seed of inspiration, that mote of a thought.
Settles in the fertile ground of my mind,
And takes root.

Growing and gathering these disparate thoughts.
Expanding and blossoming into an artisans ode,
To God's most perfect work.

But alas I must sleep.
In the scented beauty, of this new garden.
In this Eden of my own making.

A Simple Thing

Such a simple thing:
The curl of your hair on your cheek or neck;
Dappled sunlight on your skin in the awakening spring;
The way you hold your head when you daydream;
Your delicate hands resting in your lap;
The way you bite your lip when you *want* something;
How your eyes can convey such a wide range of emotion while your face remains so still;
How the shadows lite upon your curves, caressing them as a lover;
Your beautiful scent, invading my senses, enslaving me as surely as the strongest chains;
How you can still me and stop me with a single glance;
How when I look at you I can *feel* your beauty;
It is as if I am looking upon heaven itself;
Such a simple and wondrous thing;

A Touch is as a Dream

I love kissing you.
Touching you,
Looking into those amazing eyes,
Blue and Green in their turns.
Eyes I could look into forever.
You feel so amazing when we embrace.
Loving hugs to impassioned entwinements.
I cannot help but to want to lavish you with kisses.
To pleasure every inch of you with touch.
So difficult to wait,
But so very worth it.
Where every touch is as walking through the magnificence of a dream.
Your lines that I slowly trace with my fingers,
You excite me as no other.
The scent of your skin so subtle and lovely.
It draws me in.
Making me want to draw ever closer to you.
Each mystery revealed under my touch more perfect than the last.
God you are beautiful!
I am enthralled.
I can feel the radiance of your spirit,
Through your kiss, your touch, your gaze.
I cannot express how perfect you feel to me.
Both the physicality and deep within my soul.
In my deepest core you strike a chord that no other has touched.
I desire you on so many levels that its beauty amazes me.
Sitting next to you watching the rain brings me a glimpse,
A notion of heaven.
I no longer look outward to see what the world holds.
But I see that the world is right in front of me.
A woman that is worth every ounce of effort and love.
I will give all that I have.
With no question.
All that I have of myself.
I will not allow my mind to talk me out of what my heart shows me is true.

This woman, beautiful in and out, through and through.
Who makes me feel the world again.
This woman who brings me bliss with every embrace.
I will be patient for her.
I will give where she needs me to give.
I will take what she offers me to take.
I will accept her as she is.
I will make no preconceptions of her love.
And I will live where each touch is as a dream.

A Walk Through the Marshes

A walk through the marshes,
As they used to say.
A walk in the beauty of that humid place.
The coolness of those waters.
Far from the dust and heat that is our reality.
The grace of your form astounds me.
You move as sleek and sure as a lioness.
You stop and look back at me.
Beauty in every facet of that stunning face.
Shimmering black hair,
Raven hued in the dappled sunlight.
That wicked sword of a smile.
Severing reason with the slightest of touches.
You say that I should lay my bounty upon your altar.
As the curtains are opened,
The veil lifted.
Your hips, taught and tight under the supplications of my touch.
I enter the marsh and all of its beauty.
Submerge myself in its depths.
Your every line speaks the words of divinity to me.
Your body moves as the serpent over still waters.
The touch of my hand against your flesh,
As sensitive and knowing as a lovers kiss.
I feel all of you.
The response of every fiber to the worshipping attention of my touch.
One hand exploring the utter sensuality of the curve of your back.
That arch built by desire.
The other slides under.
The sacred beauty of the womb.
Feeling those soft and tender undulations.
Silken skin.
I dip my fingers in those fragrant waters.
Taste of the Lotus you say.
That slow and glorious journey,
As my fingers trace that delicate line from your love,

Across the gloried altar of your being.
Gathering in the softness of your womanhood.
Hardened points gathered between my fingers,
As a harvester tests the grain of the wheat.
I gather your lustrous hair in my grip.
Pulling you up and back to me.
Closer so you may hear my prayers.
The line of your neck, throat exposed.
Your sounds are of the sweetest music.
I kiss your neck.
The thrum of blood through wetted vein against my lips.
I say my words of worship into the ear of the Goddess.
I say them with a loud and strong voice.
I sacrifice my body and soul upon this altar.
And then we fall away.
Slipping under the surface.
The ecstasy of prayers gone answered.
Floating away from the dream.
Till our next walk through the marshes.

ADDICTION

I can feel you burning in my veins.
Acidic desires destroying me from the inside out.
Thoughts and questions filling me.
Coursing like icy water through my heart.
You.
My beautiful addiction.
The thing I love and hate.
Both for what you do to me.
You give me a pale eyed ghost to chase.
A motivation to move forward.
Uncatchable, you slip through my fingers like smoke.
I should just as well love the moon.
Beautiful, cold, distant.
Can the heat of my sun warm your barren and scarred edifice?
Or should I burn out and fade to nothing?
Alas, we are bound by powers we do not understand.
We are tied to each other,
Gravitating to each other.
At times eclipsed,
Veiled from one another.
At others bright and full of each other's light.
But we merely exist.
And drift around each other in the eternal night.

AISII

Aisii,
with a face that exudes the innocence of a child,
and a body that is gloriously that of a woman.
Feminine form in its most powerful bounty.
With lips that beckon as love itself.
Skin, pale and soft as falling moonlight.
Sensuality drifting as smoke across opiate dreams.
What a gift to the senses
Such beautiful eyes that grasp my soul.
Another deadly sin, to envy the one that calls you lover.
I should not envy, no.
I should only praise your graceful lines,
finest of God's art.
The divinity in your sculpture.
Aisii,
Oh muse, Oh siren.
Forever stealing a piece of my mind and soul.
For what I do in these few words,
others do behind the lens,
or with gifted touch.
I hold you high as Undine that is Nadja.
Perfection of form.
But what cold sculpture can compare to warmth and heat
of such a body.
And what sculptures empty gaze can stand against yours,
that deep brown weighted gaze that can steal across the ether,
and grasp the desires of both men and women.
Aisii,
True art, that is your gift to a musing heart.

APHRODITE'S BREATH

Patience I tell myself.
Heaven awaits for me.
But I must wait for heaven.
Patience.
When my heart is overwhelming me and I want to open those floodgates.
To let loose that flood of love and desire.
I must wait for her patiently.
When you want something so much that you are afraid to accept it as real.
That the reality might fade before you if you look too close.
I must wait till that voice says 'come'.
Till that tender flesh is under my hand.
Till I taste those sweetened lips.
Till reality is wrapped around me like Aphrodite's breath.
When that gaze pierces my soul as only it can.
Then I will know this is not a dream.

Burn it Away

I tried to burn my hate away, where the coals and cinders lay.
While the ashes fall from the devil's maw and I found there was hell to pay.

When I tried to drown it with that poison so familiar, all I found was the bittersweet taste.
That of dreams gone by and years of waste.

And then I tried to wash it away, but the waters found no home.
My heart was an empty chamber where hate sat all alone.

Where do I find redemption, to pry my heart open wide?
When shall I accept love, when it feels like suicide?

When shall I escape the prison my mind keeps me trapped inside?
When will I touch my fate and when will I die?

When do I let slip my dreams, like dust into the sky?
How shall I accept the life, that now I can only decry?

My heart wants only desire; my mind wants the truth in the strife.
My body wants to feel; my soul yearns for the next life.

How long when these are gone till my powers cease to burn bright?
And age and illness extinguish my light.

Those things I need so deeply are the things that drive me mad.
For when I reach out for what is good, I withdraw for what may be bad.

Is it so wrong to dream of my end?
Deaths loving embrace to which we all are sent?

There is something deep within me, something that needs to be fed.
My secret, is it my strength, or my weakness instead?

Spilling my emotions on pages with ink.
Pondering my end and toeing the brink.

Wondering if my future is what God has in store.
Or if I have passed my use and forever shut the door.

Is there a purpose, a meaning, some glorious end?
Or a slow repose, weak, broke, and bent.

Have the loves of my life come, gone, and went?
Or is there another around some unseen bend.

How long to suffer the liars and fools.
Count me amongst them, my self-destructions own tool.

Filled full of anger, distrust and self-doubt.
Desires and lusts that toss me about.

Every day wondering if this is heaven or hell.
How to know which side of Karma I'm on, if only I could tell?

Am I suffering for transgressions or are my wounds freshly healed?
A new taxation of the soul or one newly repealed.

When will I know these things, oh when will I know?
In heaven or hell, or grave deep and cold?

BUTTON AND CLASP

I look at her and my mind is captivated.
Beauty!
A face that draws desire out of men, and women.
Her long curling locks resting against the tender skin of her neck.
Gracing the line of her face.
Her clothes accentuate the beauty of her body so very well.
In cut, form, and fashion.
The V of her blouse showing just enough to engage the curious mind.
What lies under that next button?
What does she look like beneath that sleek fabric?
What would she feel like under my hands?
What glorious mysteries would be revealed, one after the other?
Under button and clasp.
What taught lines would pass beneath my fingers?
What soft and yielding flesh would gain the deepest of my attentions?
I wonder what she would smell like.
Not the perfume or other ends.
But that close up scent, intense with heat.
The scent of her in bloom.
What heaven would be seen from lover's angles?
What rapturous scenes would unfold as I turn and pull her?
Moving her to those tried and true machinations of love?
What sounds could I invoke under my touch and taste?
If only I had days to spend on her every curve.
Every texture and tenseness.
There is nothing greater than feeling a woman melt under your tongue.
No reward, no greater glory.
Gripping her hips and pulling her in.
What heaven is there but this?
What would it be like to feel every inch of her?
To feel that softness of inner thigh as I open those doors,
Those gates to the Temple of the Goddess.
Or to see the smooth lines of her back,
And how they move as she clenches her hands against the sheets.
What would she look like at that moment of climax?

To look into her eyes at that primal moment.
The dilation of her eyes, letting in the light of God.
How the color of her eyes would change.
Denser and deeper.
Will that mystery be as beautiful as I imagine it will be?
Will a blush grace that smooth and lovely cheek?
What will the sound of her heart be?
What will it feel like against my lips as I kiss her neck?
As I kiss her wrist, her breasts, her belly?
As I trace that V from her hips to her pleasure with my kisses?
To feel that heat from her body?
Radiant as the sun.
We look up and catch each other's eye, and smile.
You have that smile and look that tell me you know what I have been thinking.
We smile a little bit wider.
You can tell I look at you with the respect of a mortal man,
Beholding the visage of a Goddess.
That when I see you I see the beauty and awesome power of the feminine form.
That lies under button and clasp.

CONCENTRATION CAMP IN THE SOUL

There is a concentration camp in my soul.
That is where my love must go.
When again shall it be free?
When again, she'll love me.

DARK MISTRESS

My dark mistress,
You are with me again.
I had another.
A true and good woman.
But perhaps I missed you too much.
Perhaps I wanted you more.
Though you are no mortal being.
You are, to many, emptiness and loneliness.
But you love me, and I you, in your darkness.
Always you wait there for me.
Always loving and ever patient.
You are comfort to me.
You will never hurt me.
Though you are cold as night.
You are, Alone.
Blackest locks against pale skin.
Lips perfect and red.
You are the welcoming embrace of darkness, emptiness.
When the heat of mortal love dissipates and is gone.
When that light surely fades.
Your hands caress my tired and weary soul.
As I lay back into your still pool.
Letting your fragrant waters soothe my tortured skin.
Your earthen scent calming as the end of a spring storm.
Pale eyed goddess of the moon.
Why do you love this human?
This flesh and bone and blood?
Is it because you know that I will always end my days with you?
In our lost garden.
In the midst of my cavernous heart.
Your lips gentle upon my skin.
Your embrace is as the dark heavens.
Your soulful light shines soft and sweet.

Lighting the night of my soul.
I lie against your fertile bosom.
As those before me have for a thousand years.
For now you acquiesce to my wanderings.
For my heated moments.
While you wait for my eternal night.
And our souls will then be forever entwined.

DEATH'S FAVORITE PRIZE

Death's favorite prize is those who endure.
More time for him to want, more time for him to adore.

Take in your hands the mothering earth.
She will accept your death as she gave you your birth.

Give her your time whether for good or for ill.
Give her your everything, before death makes you still.

The world is a cruel and daunting place.
Filled with Angel's wings and the Devil's face.

Life is not punishment but a test of grace.
You must try to conquer it before you leave this place.

Have faith in the souls of others who love you just for being.
Never give in to sorrow or stop searching for meaning.

DELILAH EFFECT

Struck low once again by the Delilah effect.
Weakened by my desires.
My armor sundered by the hope of love.
I have only now to negotiate
an uneasy peace with my soul.
To await that fatal blow.
The death of love, the death of hope.

DESERVING

We talk of the future,
of plans and wants.
We talk of living together and living apart.
We talk of all those things that lovers share.
We talk of love.

Then the blackness comes.
sliding over me in its cold caress.
I have to peer into it,
plumb its inky depths.
For I know that in it lies my faults and my sins.
My lust. My wrath. My pride.

I desire women greatly,
I desire you most of all.
Yet desire is a torch in an endless night.
It will surely burn out leaving only the dark and the cold.
You ask me of love,
the constant warmth which outlasts even the sun,
and the stars and the heavens.
And I see in my blackness only that faint glimmer of desire and want.
And I wonder.

You, you are such an incredible lover,
seemingly made of my very dreams.
Yet I feel I cannot love you enough,
or that I can give you the immensity of love that you are deserving of.

Perhaps I dug too deep when last I excised the wounds of a broken heart.
Perhaps I sowed those verdant fields with salt and fire,
so that I would not want to visit them again.
What of those ruined lands?
Can they be redeemed?
Will time truly heal all?

You are such a perfect and good woman.
You struggle as we all do,
your life has never been easy.
It has been harsher than most.
You give me everything I need.
But I lack for want.

You ask me if I love you and I say I do.
I say I do with all that I have.
But do you know how little I have left inside of me?

I would never hurt you, even though I feel that I am.
This heart, disconnected from this soul.
Smoldering ruins, darkest of caves.
I desire love and loving you.
But desire is the flame with no warmth.
My mind says love, and you are so worthy of the best of love.
But inside I feel hollow.
Adrift on the seas of time.
I can see land but I cannot reach it.

Only when I touch you and taste you do I feel some semblance of life.
Those sounds you make, moans and soft sighs, screams and passionate words.
I do not pull away from your nails digging in at the end,
because that feeling reminds me that I am still here, a ghost no more.

Do I tell you these words?
I feel I would hurt you with them,
yet I feel I would hurt you by feigning greater love that is not real.
Is it not enough that I hold you above all other women?
Is it not enough that I seek your companionship?
Is it not enough that I would give and take life for you?
I ask this not of you, but of myself.
Am I deserving of you?
Am I deserving of the love I see in your eyes,
of the love I hear in your words and taste on your lips?
Am I deserving of the pleasures of your body?
How long shall I stand in the ashen fields of the past?
Or shall I reap what I have sown?

Am I indeed the cavernous one?
Infinite in darkness and scope.
Or do I fear you?
Do I fear giving myself to such a woman as you?
Would I rather face an uncertain future?
Would I rather want for a woman's graces and not have them,
though if I had those wet embraces I would feel no true love in return.
Would I pass you by?

Would I stand in the barren plain wishing the future and regretting the past?
For now I will, I must, give you all that this shell of a vessel holds.
Though I feel the pain of one who knows that his best is surely not enough.

DREAM

I woke up this morning with your scent upon my senses.
But you are here for such a little time, and have been gone for so much longer.
I can feel your presence in the stillness of this morning.
Though you are where, I know not.
The bed contains the warmth of two, but one is its only companion.
Were you here my love?
Were you with me in my dreams?
Did our moment of want collide on some uncharted plane, some ether world.
Do you sense me on this morning as I sense you?
Do you pull your pillow close hoping to save that ghostly perfume?
Do you wonder if I am wondering of you?
Wondering of the wonder of it?
Our moments have been deep and pure.
Though we knew that it would be momentary, we loved unrestrained.
We are far apart but we can touch and sense and love, in our dreams.
The bed is cold now, overwhelmed by the harsh light of day.
But I carry that ember in my heart through the coldness waiting for the next igniting breath to bring you back my way.

DREAMING DREAMS

Dreaming dreams,
of the past and future.
Of the sweetened scent of skin,
of nails digging in.
Awakening to cold reality,
which world to be in?

EMPTY

I see you again,
But I feel nothing.
I watch you with no more remorse or feeling,
Than watching a leaf float down river.
You are still undeniably beautiful to me,
But the desire has gone.
My heart frozen over,
Solid, unfeeling.
Dead as Winter.

Perhaps one day it shall see that spring again,
But with another.
We have seen our season in the sun.
I seek now a gentle and constant woman.
To not be burned by the flame,
But enveloped by a dream.
A woman with a soft soul,
Unangry with the world.
A woman who wants to be a woman.
Secure in her feminine powers.

To see the death of this love,
Not with hate, but of indifference.
And not even saddened by the surety of its loss.
I am empty.

FALL ON YOUR SWORD

Let that cool blade slip effortlessly between my ribs.
To pierce that fiery cauldron, and deliver me from its desires.
Murder my anguish.
But no,
As I lean there slumped against the sword of my own making.
My heart still beats.
Clasped around that steel like a lovers embrace.
My heart does not wish to end,
What my mind wants destroyed.
I want an end that will not come.
Or do I?
The dichotomy of man does not end at his desire to create and destroy.
Heart, soul and mind in constant conflict.
Periods of peace disrupted by utter torment.
So I pull the blade back out, slowly.
Feeling my heart pound against it.
The tip of the blade exits and falls to the earth.
And I let go of the haft as I cannot let go of the love that brought me here.
And let it fall back to the dust.
But I know I shall be here again,
To lift that weighted sting.
And fall again in this eternal fight.

FEARLESS LOVE

When I am near you,
When I think of you,
When I look into those beautiful eyes.
You give me a sense of fearless love.

Though we have both been through a lot,
I am going to love you like you are my first love,
and I will love you as if you are my last love.

First Night

I slept little last night.
The first time I have touched your soft skin.
How could I slumber feeling your softness without,
and desiring your softness within.

So long since I have enjoyed a woman's touch.
Felt the fullness of your lips.
The swell of your breasts.
The curve of your hips.

I could not waste these first new hours with you.
Just touching and feeling and kissing until the night is through.
As I think back sitting in fluorescent glare.
Remembering your soft sounds and silken hair.

Your scent wraps around me lingering upon my skin.
Eros's ether soaking in.
My every breath filled with memoried touch.
Igniting my senses with electric rush.

Blood warmed by increasing fire.
An enraptured embrace of desire.
Now I wait for the next time together.
To enter within and lay my love,
on dew soaked heather.

First Taste

Your kisses are greater than poet's words.
Your touch greater than sweetest song.
Your eyes more beautiful than precious gems.
Your love stronger than the strongest of storms.

Your scent lingers upon my skin.
Your taste upon my lips.
My fingertips dream of your soft skin.
My soul warms to think of your radiant beauty.

FOR ONE LOST

Yes, this latest love was strong, not only with emotion but with reason.
Passionate, but with purpose.
Though I didn't show it very well.
She was and is a woman worth my every effort.
The kind of woman that fulfills every need and want a man can have.
She should always know that about herself.
That she can bring out the finest qualities in a man.
She just has to give them some time to realize it for themselves.
Some say to live only in the present.
But the present is fleeting and slips quickly into the past, without the permanence of hope in the future.
A very few women are worth the trouble of winning and losing.
This blue eyed girl will always be the best thing that ever happened to me.
It takes a damn fine woman to make a man wax poetic.
The kind of woman that can pull those words from the guarded depths.
The kind of woman you never regret loving or losing, because she was worth every last moment of both.
The kind of woman you love forever.
Good night to those beautiful blue eyes.
I love you the same together or apart.
Even if we are apart forever you will always have the best part of me.
All these words are said with the awe and admiration of what you inspire in me.
There is no sadness or anger or weakness behind them.
Only the strength that comes from a better man for loving you.
There are some people that have the quality of greatness about them.
Something innate and radiant that you can feel a mile away.
Take my advice, however belatedly I acquired it. If you feel that way about someone let them know it every day.
I often feel as if my words are like coins tossed into a wishing well, with only blackness and silence in return.
I would rather hear the worst of things than the utter cacophony of silence.
I expect nothing substantial but absolute nothingness is too much.
Was there any emotion behind these past weeks?
Or was it just that prized emotionlessness.

Is it such a hard thing to do to tell me the truth of what you have felt, to someone who would never hurt you or violate the trust of your confidence?

Did I truly hurt you, or was it some instantaneous disconnect?

Could I have stopped it?

Can I?

Was it easy to make that break, or did you have to convince yourself?

Did you have to talk yourself out of loving me?

This is what I need to know.

I would rather know the reality of it than the thousand versions of the truth my mind can conjure.

You are as a blank screen.

Is there indifference behind it, hidden pain, sorrow, cold logic?

I can never tell without you telling me.

At least we still speak on occasion.

And that is enough to get me by, even though you never speak of your feelings or thoughts.

I still think about you and love you every minute of every day.

I wonder about you, I worry about you.

FOR PEARL-DUST

Reading your words, a glimpse of your soul.
Powerful, emotional, squeezing my heart.
Such a feeling is that feeling.
One which I feel so seldom now.
That feeling.
Such a physical sensation, yet inspired and derived from the depths of heart and mind.
Your words bring me there just as surely as if I were in your mind's eye at that very instance.
Floating like a mote in fading light.
Yet I will never know but a fraction of the emotional power of these recounted events.
Never to plumb the depths of your storied soul.
Who are you?
What makes you who you are?
What are your wants?
What are your desires?
Do I want or need to know?
Or is it that your words are food for a starving wolf of a heart.
And that heart, this wolf, wishes to feed.
To gain sustenance from revealed love, pain, sorrow, and joy.
Your poems like blood spilt out across the page.
An image of your words as if they are your heart held in outstretched hands.
Offering the world a chance to glimpse its unutterable beauty.
I crave your inspired words to fill the empty chasm that is my heart.
So I slink back to my empty den.
And watch and wait for that next anticipated meal.
And dream of such warmth as that exuded by your lovely words.

FREE

Pacing the ground as a caged animal.
Trapped within the iron edifice of my own mind.
I feel that one day I will be free of myself.
Free of this shell.
I have always felt I was contained.
That there is something inside of me.
Waiting to be free.
But what is it?
What resides within me?
Is it something good and beautiful?
Or am I opening the gates of my own personal hell?
I want to know.
And I don't fear it.
Regardless of its consequences.
But is this thing,
This compulsion,
This desire,
Going to destroy me?
Or even worse,
Destroy those I love?
Would that I knew!
But would I care?
Yes.
But for a very, very few.
My own blood.
Maybe one or two more.
Those that entered me and took my soul.
Claimed my blood.
Those that I love as I love the proof of my own flesh.
Yes.
Those precious few.
But what if I unleash fire?
Would I dare expose them to the flame?
I would not.
That would be the end.

The end of me.
Destroy myself before the world.
What would be lost but an empty shell?
The love I have for them is indestructible.
But my mind is fallible.
I will find my end.
But not in this cage.
I will be free when I die.
For good or ill.
But I will die free.
Unfettered.
Looking death in the eyes.
Even if it is alone.

How I Love Thee

How I love thee, as they say.
A gaze to shake the souls of men.
Holding the gentle curves of your face in my hands.
The feeling of our lips when they touch.
The heat from your skin.
The way you give my touch purpose.
Your voice gives me peace.
You are Woman, Goddess, Heaven, Eternity, for me.
A moment in your presence is infinite to my soul.
That beauty inside you shows me a purity I can never know.
No other can capture me so.
Captivate me with mere presence.
You make me want a love that I have never known.
You in a moment can give me more than I have known in a lifetime.
That glimpse of Elysium, Paradise.
A Valkyrie for my stormy soul.

I SHALL SEE

I Shall See,

What is the sun without the moon?
Both with the beauty of their light.
For without the sun there is no light,
And without the moon no place for it to rest its prodigious glow.

What is the night without day?
Both with the beauty of their time.
Would we lack the night?
Filled with its honeysuckle breezes and lover's embraces.
Would we forego the sun and its treasures?
To miss its glory upon a lover's face.

We are so different you and I.
So different, yet with similarities also.
Your eyes, so beautiful, lock me in place.
I should say so to you,
But your gaze stills me and silences me.
All I can do is look into them,
I cannot speak.
Reason is stolen from me by those pale pools.

You are steady in your ways.
Strong with vigor and sass.
And I await your touch.
What wonders it will bring.
I memorize the lithe curves of your body as you walk.
The shape and subtleties of your hands.

The timbre of your voice.
What will it be like to take those nimble and delicate hands in mine?
To kiss those wrists to feel a quickened heart beat?
To taste those lips?
To wrap you in my arms?
To feel your sweetened embrace?

But I must be patient.
As good things come to those who wait.
I want to experience all you have to offer.
To wade into the waters of your life.
To see your passions.
To walk beside you in this life.
To gaze upon your moonlit face.
To see the suns golden kiss upon it.
You fascinate me.
You intrigue me.

What will the future hold?
I ask myself not.
The future will be revealed in its own time.
I cannot prejudge it.
I cannot force my will upon it.
Lest it collapse as some ether dream.
I can only accept this God given path.
To step upon it bravely.
To walk forward into that blessed unknown.
What heavenly bounty awaits?
I shall see.
With patience and grace I shall wait.
And I shall see.

If Only

You don't want to be with me,
But you don't want to be without me.
Am I your safe bet?
Am I your safety net?
Always there to catch you if you fall.
Even though we are too different,
In our ways and wants.
When it is just you and I,
Together, alone.
And the world is no more.
Where there is nothing but our love between us.
That is where we are one.
Where nothing and no one else matters.
I am not your idea of perfect.
In form or function.
But you know my love is real, and strong.
And only for you.
If only that was all that mattered in this life.
If we could be alone in a world,
Made out of nothing but our love for each other.
If only that was all that mattered.

INTOXICATED

You are beautiful.
Your taste is as the finest wine.
You intoxicate me.
You lift me from this dreary world.
I drown in those deep blue eyes.
Delivering me from my mortal fate.
What method of men could bring me pleasure,
More than the drinking from you.
A second in your presence is as a night of strong liquor.
Yet it sustains me for days.
So easy to slip into addiction with you.
My beautiful dream.
You infiltrate me,
Destroy me.
Yet I cannot turn away from you.
I cannot resist raising you to my lips.
I cannot put you down.
I cannot stop wanting to feel you coursing through my veins.
Deliver me from reason.
Let me rest in your heavens.
Give me solace in your paradise.
Burn me,
Sacrifice me upon your altar.
Consume me.
Rend me from this pallid existence.
For a single vision of you,
Leaves this world as a hell without you.
My beautiful nectar.
Deliver me.

KISS ME TOUCH ME

Kiss me lips and bedroom eyes.
Touch me skin and take me thighs.
These and others are things that tell my hands to tell my mind,
This is what perfect feels like.

LET ME BE

Why must you draw the hatred out of me?
Why must you pull that venom from its resting place?
Why must you disturb its dangerous placidity?
I am like a landmine, harmless unless stepped on.
Yet you are there, tapping on my hardened case.
Why must you toss the rocks of vile remarks into that still black pool?
Why must you raise demons from the depths where they have lain still
for so long?
I want only to love those whose beauty is art.
I want to mourn the one I have lost.
Not to waste my time on your petty and hateful manner.
Once I counted you among friends with highest respect.
Now you are lower than a dog to me, because dogs at least know loyalty.
I am blank of countenance as you are being so unkind.
But in my head my blades unwind.
I am tired by your spitefulness.
Yet I cannot escape.
Let me be.

LINGERING BEAUTY

Your scent lingers on my skin,
Reminding me of what has been.
Glittering eyes and beautiful face,
And the rhythm of your pace.
Your spice remains upon my lips,
Whence from your cup did I sip.
Memories of our tangled throes,
Surest targets of Cupid's bow.
Your wetness soaks my searching touch,
No such thing as far too much.
Yes your pleasure springs upon my lips,
Heaven holds not such as this.

MEDUSA'S GAZE

You approach.
As I stand behind my high walls.
Armor on, weapons ready, my defenses up.
I know the danger even as I let you close.
Am I so trusting of my own powers against such as yours?
We speak, such banal and simple words.
Then I catch your glance, those eyes.
Piercing, cool, turning me to stone as surely as Medusa's gaze.
Why do I do this?
Invite this?
Knowing the danger, and letting the distance shrink still.
Ever closer.
Is it because I desire so much to be near that warm and dangerous skin?
To feel your heat instead of the cold plates against my heart?
A moth to the flame.
You cloud me in the opiate of your being.
Whether you want to, or know it, is of no consequence.
Then, so subtle as to be unnoticed, so clever, so very slowly.
Your blade of heartache slips under my armor.
Always finding the weakness.
And finding its mark, digs deep.
You slowly fade back from whence you came.
My sorrow and desire masking all.
You are gone again.
Then the dawning realization.
I am bled out from your hidden wound,
Before I even realize it is there.
Before you distant form is beyond my sight.
And then, alone, I drop to my knees.
Insanguinated.
Hollowed out, pulling me down to where I belong.
How can I endure this?
Embracing that cold blade just to feel your touch once again.
Is that pain so much better than no feeling at all?
Would I suffer the humiliation of weakness,

Just to feel the awesome power of your gaze?
What use this armor?
Shining, hard, useless.
These walls high and thick?
With their gates always ready to be thrown open.
What use this heart?
This ruined patchwork target for your sure arrows.
What use this fortitude?
That desires your torture as if it was your love.
Will I ever be free of you?
Will I ever desire to be free of you,
More than I desire your gilded chains?
Will I ever desire anyone more than you?
Desire anything more than you?
Or shall I suffer eternally,
And willingly,
Under Medusa's gaze?

MOMENTARY MUSE

I should be working but instead I dreamed. A sight becomes a muse in my mind.

Suffer the day
growing old slowly, mercilessly.
Wasted time
wanting only to behold the feminine beauty,
drifting through the streets, the shops, the dreams.

Is it not natural that those carriers of life and love,
should draw me so strongly
from decaying time.
Their looks and words like warm water
over a heart frozen by endless tedium.

Most beautiful of arts,
most powerful of nature,
hottest of desires.
To be burnt and frozen
with that single glance
that look of looks
woman is perfect as woman.

OF DEATH AND LIFE

I encountered death today.
At first there was sorrow, surprisingly deep and painful, as I knew her little.
But her words had struck me and drew on my empathy and my sympathy.
To lose another voice, and such a lucid and powerfully emotional one.
Through the day my thoughts have shifted.
Nothing had the power to interest me or move my soul.
Restless and aching, my mind flitted from one thing to another.
Concentration slipping away to blurred inattentiveness.
Then my heart in its emotional distress turned my mind to another.
To her.
How I need a woman's touch right now.
How I need to be with a woman tonight.
To make love to her.
Why this sudden need?
Was it something innate and primal?
To meet death with the mingling of life?
Or is it merely a distraction?
Something to pull me away from the pain and despair in my heart?
Sorrow for the one lost.
Am I trying to avoid the loss by gaining her?
By filling her?
Trying to side step the cold hand of death by touching her warmth?
My heart is wrenched by the knowledge that somewhere across the vast ocean a life has been extinguished.
Yet I try to ignite another candle in its place.
To feel the warmth and glow against the shell of a darkened heart.
Even still the scent of that flame undone fills the chamber of my mind.
Why do I feel I must weep?
Is it something deeper?
Did I indeed love this person in such a profound way that I didn't even recognize it?
Have I truly learned that I can love a person as blood even though our only contact was through the godlessness of a machine?
To have shared so little of our lives with each other, maybe a few hours all told.

Was your emotion such a power as to transcend that hurried ether world and touch my soul?

Yes, that is it.

I have learned that love has many faces and no face at all.

As God embraces you and comforts you as none of us could, I feel I must embrace a woman, that thing God has given man to let him know what paradise is like.

That act which in one is the truest and most human act and also the glimpse of God's grace.

I loved her though I knew her so little.

Now I must love another to assuage that loss that has sundered my heart so surely.

Death waits for us all, but for now, there is life.

OF SEASONS AND WOMEN

Fierce summer,
weighing down on the mind.
Oppressive heat,
Humid suffocation of my thoughts.
Hard to breathe,
hard to sleep.
My drifts to thoughts of a crisp autumn day.
Cool wind whipping bright leaves around my feet.
Or to the beauty of snow fall at night,
and the beauty of sun glinting off snow fields in the morning.
The deep greens, browns, and blacks of a rainy spring day.
Walking beneath the trees,
black soft soil under my feet.
Varied hues of green always drawing the eye deeper.
The patter of a soft rain against the leaves the only sound.

But summer holds no want for me.
Hemmed in by the thick dull green,
and the hazy heat.
Heavy breezes hum against my tripwire.
When even the night cannot placate the unease of my mind.
A long day in the sun.
Sun sears the skin.
Hard work on hard days.
I walk into the bedroom.
You are lying naked on the sheets.
Sweat glistening on your covers.
Trickling as a stream into your valleys.
I drink from my iced glass,
and lay the coolness of my kiss upon your breasts.
Your skin is hot and deeply salted.
I am overcome with desire at that taste.
Why, I do not know.
You hesitate,
it is unbelievably hot.

But you kiss me,
and taste of my salt.
We are soon embraced.
Fast, aggressive.
The tripwire is sprung.
Then it is over.
If only a kind breeze to cool our skin.
No more holding lovers close.
Lying apart to dissipate the heat that needs no sun.
A new morning.
Already hot.
For now greeted only by the unending hordes of insects,
the choking mix of pollen and mold.
Then the arid heat of August.
That time of rain dances,
when even the sky loses it blue brilliance.

But then the loving embrace of autumn.
Wet, but a clean moistness.
The gray powdered earth drinking in the cool rains.
This is when the forest beckons.
The air is cooler now under the trees.
The danger has lessened.
The cool weather has sent the more fell creatures slithering back to ground.
Leaves, yellow, orange, red, purple,
lie softly on the ground in the cool shadows.
Soil becoming black again,
covered in the deep green of moss,
tinged now in mint,
before the winter lays it to rest.
That earthy smell that compels a primal quickness in my heart.
The house smells of spices.
It is cool enough to bake again you said with a smile.
When home was home,
and all I wanted was to come home to you.
The rustle of leaves through the open window.
You stand at the sink,
I wrap my arms around you,
pulling close.

Kissing your neck behind the ear.
This is bliss, heaven, paradise.
The moment I was put on this earth to experience.
I lead you to the bedroom.
Cool breeze,
and the dry softness of your skin.
The warmth of it against me.
Your smile, your kisses.
The heady scent of your perfume.
That close in scent, subtle.
Meant for me alone.

Autumn falls to winter.
Sycamore and Ash leading the way.
Black fingers over my head as I step through the snow.
The crush of my boot through the thin crust, sinking in.
That silence of the winter forest.
The smell of the wood smoke that drifts like ghosts.
Tracing through the solemn watch of the Oaks.
The feel of ancient Gods is here.
The weighted branches of fragrant Pine and Cedar.
And I know that the feeling of this is shared by others across this great world.
I only wish to see the wolves again.
Of those days of youth when I shared these woods with them.
Perhaps I shall see them again.
Once I meet my end.
I do so love the snow on a winters walk.
Snow falling softly in the hushed silence.
Just sitting quietly listening to winter's voice.
I walk into the house and shake off my coat.
You stand there silhouetted by the flames of the stove.
A woman's heat is the only relief of winter.
I warm my hands by the fire.
Then I place their warmth on your cheek and neck.
What comfort is the warmth of your kiss.
When it is not the covers,
but what is beneath,

that warms the nights.
It is cold under the covers at first.
But not for long.
Soon we are comforted by a warmth that will last the night.

Winter's blacks and tans soon lose their icy grip.
The sun marches north.
That day when your hardened eyes light upon that first bud,
that first blade of grass.
My family tradition of spring,
the boys giving the first flowers of springs to all the women at the house.
The sun's brightness matching the flame that is once again lit in your soul.
Rain turns from cruel and cold to cool and pleasant.
Winds whip up in their frantic dance.
Storms dance across the broad landscape.
Then those calm, soft, slow, rainy days.
Shoots turn the earth.
The scent of earth and winters leaves overturned.
That peculiar joy of winters end.
The girls in their spring dresses.
That perfect warmth when the sun shines down without winter's thieving hand.
I look at you.
So beautiful in the dappled sunlight.
My hand rests on the hem of your sundress.
Half on that light fabric,
half on the sun warmed skin of your thigh.
Your smile, your eyes.
Your skin warm against my kiss and touch.
Sunlight revealing your glory.
And those quiet mornings.
Rain against the roof.
Slow and steady.
The distant rumble of thunder.
The comforting darkness of a late spring morning.
Bird songs sweeten the air.
Cool air and the warmth of your magnificence.

The breeze carries your scent mingled with that of the rain,
as the angels with their censers.

And once again I am here.
In the present.
Early summer.
Hot and wet.
While these traits are good in lovers,
they leave much to be desired in the weather.

OF SERAPHIM AND NEPHALIM

It is midnight.
I lay here caressing your delicate lines with my fingers.
Memorizing the unique facets of your Self.
You fascinate me.
Enthrall me.
No two women are the same.
All beautiful in their own fashion.
I love you now, as I love them all.
When I cup your angelic face in my hands,
It is as a vision of heaven to my senses.
My touch 'sees' you.
I feel your beauty emanate from within.
Radiant.
I bask in the glory of it.
So many times I ask myself,
What is it that I desire from a woman?
So many times that has eluded me.
But tonight I know.
I want to feel the power of a pagan goddess!
I want to feel the fertile heat against my soil.
I want a woman that is worthy of worship.
I do my part.
I lay myself at your altar.
I let myself be consumed.
That is what I want most.
To be enfolded by those fires.
Burnt to embers and carried unto heaven by your passions.
Sweetest oblivion.
I lay here.
The scent of tuberose and honeysuckle drift on moistened air.
How beautiful you are.
How beautiful the woman.
I lose myself in your glorious art.
I spend hours touching and tasting.
All those varied textures and tastes, subtle flavors.

Visions of heaven entrained in my mind forever.
No words of man can truly describe what I see and feel.
Are there angelic tomes devoted to this subject?
Seraphim and Nephalim.
When even those godly beasts can be seduced by the powers of women.
How can I say what brought those guardians to their knees.
Why heaven is on earth for some.
Is that also why I am cursed?
That I am drawn too closely to those worldly pleasures.
Instead of the reward of some divinity?
Why some that desire beckons I shun for fear of Lolita's end?
To spare them my fervent worship.
Why I cannot be with a woman while these desires shred my soul.
Looking for that ancient power in a single mortal vessel.
But I love you all so.
Some whose faces captivate me.
Indeed such as that I remember only the face,
the eyes, the lips, the voice.
That intangible something.
Some whose bodies inflame my desire where others cannot.
Some whose mere words reflect their souls and enslave mine.
Some who unleash an energy so strong, so powerful, that I feel the goddess in them,
merely by entertaining the thought of them.
That magnificence.
Women that know they are women.
Masculinity does not equal power to them.
Their strength lies not in trying to be equal to men,
but in realizing that their powers surpass men's.
We are the hammer, they are the hammer smith.
We are the spear, the sword, they the guided touch.
Though I worship that life giving goddess of old,
I demand that she be worthy of it.
Loyalty demands its price.
The serenity of a woman wrapped around me.
I expect of the heavens, heaven.
I devote myself.
I will have all of her devotions.

Every inch of her magnificence.
All of its perfection against the attentions of taste and touch.
To feel the pulsations under her skin.
How better to feel?
What more sensitive meter than the tip of my tongue?
Where calloused fingers fail.
Where the palm no longer divines.
That is how I read a woman.
That is how I experience her paradise.
One day love, it shall be you.
Await.
Prepare you altar.
Be the goddess you were meant to be.
One day I will kneel before you.
You will hear my supplications.
And feast upon my offerings.
And we shall be one.
Under the night.

PART OF ME

Part of Me
My love for you is unreasonable,
It makes no sense,
Or no sense that I can make of it.
It is there, true and palpable,
But it isn't there in that it just a thought and a feeling.
My heart loves you with all its might,
But my mind knows that my heart is on a fool's errand.
I want to be near you,
But then again I don't.
It depends on who is more powerful at the time,
The heart or the mind.
Part of me wants to discard you,
Discard us.
Part of me wants to bask in every second we are together.
Part of me knows of the love we had together.
Part of me knows of the harshness we dealt to each other.
Who wins?
Who should win?
Part of me wants to fight,
To prove my love.
Part of me accepts the unrequited love you give.
Part of me wants to excise you,
Exorcise you from my soul.
Part of me wants to exalt in you.
Part of me accepts that we will never be again.
Part of me refuses to accept that end.
Part of me wants to go down a new path.
Part of me want the path to you,
No matter the tortuous terrain.
Part of me wants to never see you again.
Part of me can't wait to see you again.
Part of me accepts this defeat,
This loss of love.
Part of me wants to fight for this love forever.

Part of me wants to speak of this to your very soul.
Part of me knows I am talking to myself.
Part of me loves you.
Part of me hates you.
Part of me holds you on high.
Part of me wants to cast you down.
Part of me wants us to be whole again.
Part of me knows we will always be apart.
Part of me knows you want none of me.
Part of me knows you will always have part of me.

POISON

Poison,
Why do I let you do this to me?
I know your methods.
I would rather you give me a swift end.
Than to let me suffer your slow poison.
Why do you do this to me?
I sit unknowing.
Is it revenge for the wounds you have suffered at my hand?
Or do you like watching me twitch upon your web?
Does torturing me this way excite you?
Is that what you need?
Am I your drug?
You cut as the poppy and lick the wound?
Waiting for my blood to ooze into your cup?
Destroy me already!
Incinerate me upon your flame!
Do not laugh as I dance upon your glass!
Unable to free myself by succumbing to your destruction.
Do you not know that I love you?
Do you not understand that the truth from your lips,
No matter how harsh it is,
Is better than this death by a thousand cuts?
Let your blade rest against my chest.
Let me slide myself upon your cruel steel.
Let me be finished of you.
In my weakness I beg you to pull the trigger.
Deliver me from the beauty of your tortuous fate for me.
Allow me to step into oblivion.
Close my eyes to your angelic hues.
Let me drink all of your poison at once,
One final time.
Free me!
Burn me!
Set me free!

SEDUCE

You ask to read my words again.
I hesitate.
My words are my heart.
Would I dare to expose them?
You are deadly in both ways and means.
And I know it.
A sure and swift killer of men's hearts.

But I can feel you now.
Like heat from hammered steel.
I feel that you want to feed from me.
There is your weakness.
Your desires get the better of you.
As my passions get the better of me.
Your wants open you as a book, as a flower.
Betraying that fragile core.
If I meet with you it is I who will be doing the taking.
You will get what you desire, what you need.
I will get the sustenance for my soul.

I hand you those battered pages.
Blooded ink.
Heart and mind resurrected on the page.
You are the muse to some.
And as a woman, in a way, muse to them all.
As you read I watch the color rise on your cheek.
So beautiful!
That rose of vulnerability.
Of innocent desire lain bare.

I lose myself in watching you.
Words will never express how you make me feel.
Would it surprise you that I could spend eternity gazing at your beauty?
That magnificent edifice of God's greatest masterpiece.
You finish and fold those thoughts in your delicate hands.

Those lithe fingers that have brought me to the heavens.
So many times before.
You look at me.
THE look!
That LOOK!
No physicality could exude sex as much as that look.

I lead you to the bedroom.
So familiar to you.
Easy as a dream.
Our kiss is as the act itself.
Everything desired and wanted all at once.
I pull up your blouse.
Familiar secrets beneath.
Flesh upon flesh.
Desire upon desire.
I capture your arms with it.
Controlling you.
You fight for more contact as I pull away.
Always just a little out of reach.
You fight for the taste of my lips.
And I hold you.
Engaged but exposed.
Kissing your neck and pulling away.
Familiar games.
You move your hips against me.
What sweet and subtle sounds you make.
In your need.

Such beauty.
I set you free.
You are as an animal.
No thought or reason.
Not now.
Just feeling and instinct.
You feel so amazing against me.
Soft shimmering skin.
Men have not invented the method to say this feeling.
Maybe those words are God's secret.

I lower myself as I lower your hems.
My kiss leads the way through wonders untold.
Do you know I love you so?

In this you give me the life that nothing else can offer.
I pull away and you pull me back in return.
The bare touch of a kiss against your love and then gone again.
Sounds of heaven.
Back and forth as a tempo on the rise.
Teasing and touching.
Forging that glorious end with my fires.
Then I give you everything.
Everything.
Every ounce of my being.
All that is within me.
The skill of my tongue.
The paths of my fingers.
Grasping you to me.

Flames leap high as a smithy with steel.
You arch against me as the world ceases.
This is the only thing that matters.
The end.
Of the beginning.
We play the game again.
But my kiss is free to roam.
To seek.
To pleasure.
No better seclusion than being alone with another as one.
Blankness beyond our light.
At last our work is formed.
We against each other.
Hard and hot.
Quenched in those lovely waters.
Our efforts have unleashed.
You smile between breathes.
Those cool green eyes.
I say 'What?'
You kiss me and say,

"I thought I came here because I wanted to tell you to learn to forget me."
I ask what you came for then, what now do you want me to do?
You say "Seduce" and laugh that sweet and deadly laugh.
You wanted to read my words love.
But you really wanted to taste them for yourself.
Once again.
Touché.

Sympathy for the Moth

Masochist?
No.
Not what you are thinking.
I have no desire for physical pain.
I put myself through it out of curiosity.
Testing my limits.
No.
My masochism is of the mental kind.
Always putting myself in the line of fire.
I know I am putting myself in the position to be hurt.
And to be hurt by the ones I love the most.
And I do it anyway.
Better the pain than nothing at all.
Wanting your touch,
Even if that touch is to rip out my heart.
That is one thing I can always be sure of.
That whenever my heart is too big,
Too full.
There will always be someone there to pull it out,
And hand it back in smaller pieces.
I would rather the blade than the silence.
Am I trying to allow you to hurt me so,
So that I can stop loving you?
Though my heart refills with love every time I look into your eyes.
I look for a wound so severe,
As to rend this vessel forever.
To empty me.
Leave me dry and broken.
Hollow.
Compelled to destroy myself with you.
To draw close to that flame.
My sympathies for the moth.
No hook or needle can savage me as your ways.
You know not what you do.
As the storm knows not the destruction that it sows.

You just sweep across the barren plain of my soul.
You are a storm.
I am the afterthought.
Merely the detritus in the path of your oblivion.
But I do so love to watch the storm rolling in.
Fascinated by its power.
Its beauty.
Its fierceness.
Whipped by your winds and rains.
But at least then I can feel.
Better that than the deadly still of loneliness.
This is what I crave,
I need,
I desire,
To feel your pain.
Because I cannot feel your love.
To burn in your fire.
Just to see your light.
I fear not this torturous existence.
No.
But I have sympathy for the moth.

THE GATES OF EDEN

What is she?
Is she the one?
Is she a way to pass the time?
Is she just a safe bet?
If she was she wouldn't affect you so.
You think of her day and night.
The sound of her voice or the thought of her beauty bring you a peace
beyond anything else you could know.
The thought of touching her is as heaven.
The question is if heaven is real.
Or is it a figment of your imagination?
Would you really give all to be with her?
Or is it just a nice idea to supplicate your mind?
She may love you.
But she will not show you that part of her soul again.
The gates of Eden are shut.
Or is this your meteoric fall?
The burning embers of your ability to love lighting the fall to destruction.
Is she your last chance?
The only chance you are willing to take?
Or is she the only chance worth taking?
Are you just a masochist for emotional pain?
Is that the only thing that feels real to you anymore?
Would you rather suffer than risk?
Or is this love real and true?
And you are trying to justify a reason to destroy it.
To free yourself from the burden of hope.
You would rather feel the alkaline and ashy heat against your flesh,
Than the succor of a heaven you can never touch.
You would rather feel the piercing blade pass through your heart,
Than submit to the fullness that can never be embraced.
But you cannot stop loving.
That love means more to you than life itself.
It is your reason for being.
What would you be without your love for her?

An empty shell, lifeless and barren?
An echo of the man she makes you want to be?
But in the end you know it is just an unrealized dream.
Heaven does not wait for you.
You walk not in hell, but in oblivion.
Nothing awaits you and you await nothing.
The abyss of your remaining time on earth resonates in your mind.
Hollow, unending.
There is no color, no blue.
Accept your end.
It is all that has ever awaited you.
You will meet your fate alone.
And rejoice.

THE WELL

Take of me what you will.
Drink from my cup as I shall drink from you.
Drench my soul's fire with a drink of your cool well.
Let my eyes rest on the gentle pools of your loving eyes.
Your dark tresses shield my skin, burnt by the glare of an unforgiving world.
Soft locks caressing my face and burdened shoulders.
My coarse and roughened face cradled in your delicate hands.
Your lips deliver me from all of my pain.
White angelic kisses soothing the cold black of a sorrowed heart.
Grace my lips with your fragrant waters.
Let me embrace you with the tide of my adoration.
Allow me to worship at that most sacred alter.
I would lift you with that ether, embrace you with it.
Give of myself all that I have.
This body, blood, and life.
All that I have though it is not enough.
What sacrifice is great enough in the heart of a man to be worthy of you, God's greatest creation?
You work of art, act of nature, haunter of dreams.
Let me fill that well of which you have let my slack my thirst.
So after hard days, cruel lonely days, I may return to it again.

Through Destruction, New Life

We always seem to find ourselves 180 degrees out from one another in our relationship.

One loving deeply, the other loving not, or with ambivalence, at the least.

Always coming to each other, passing for that brief time, and then flying off into the darkness.

We are like two colliding galaxies spinning together in a beautiful dance of death.

Coming together and then casting each other off, but always ending closer than we were before.

Until one day this tightening spiral climaxes into that anticipated explosion.

All those differing components of our souls meeting and mixing.

Destroying our old selves to become one.

Together.

To a Woman

The tangle of arms in the morning light, protective frame around your gentle being.

Your breast filling the cup of my hand.

That lovely point gracing the center of my palm.

Your perfumed hair so soft against the harsh mask of my face.

Cradled hips, the graceful lines of a woman's body.

I worship your radiant warmth as the ancients worshipped the sun.

I lay there in awe of God's greatest creation.

The rise and fall of your breaths a comforting lullaby.

The beautiful line of your jaw, though jaw seems much to coarse of a word.

Those incredible eyes.

Those delicate lobes with the single curl of hair falling on your smooth skin so beautifully.

I kiss your neck on that familiar place so I can feel your heartbeat against my lips.

In this half light, so quiet, I love you.

If not in the daylight world, then in the eternity of my soul.

To be the Assassin of the Heart

To be the assassin of one's own heart.
To decide whether to let this newfound
ability to love remain, starving.
Or let it slip back into the black abyss
from whence it came.

But no,
That love, that delicate fragile bloom must not die.
It should be cared for, nurtured,
so that one day it shall unfurl,
and show the world its true beauty.

To a Lover

Emotion grasps my heart,
pulling me towards that abyss.
How your presence would soothe my soul.
How your touch would mend this savaged heart.

To focus my being upon your soft skin.
To forget myself upon your lips.
I need you now,
I need you so.

My mind seeks you over seeming expanse.
Nothing on earth or in the heavens means as much to me now,
as having you against my hand.
To pour my cauldron against your earth.

I want to kiss you now with desire,
strongly and deeply.
What treasure means more to me now,
than the softness of your hair against my chest?

You and I alone in the darkness of the mind.
Entwined with every ounce of our beings.
How I need you!
Would you need me so?

When I am not hard and reserved,
but tender with emotion.
When every inch of your body seems my salvation.
The sound of your breath more important than the reality of my own.

The thought of your body against mine seems the greatest of glories.
Would that I had always been there for you,
when you needed me thus.
Would that I had realized and taken you in my arms.

Had I kissed those lovely lips.
Had I held that beautiful blue gaze.
Would that I had held your weakness in my strength.
Had I let your waves break upon my rock.

We are near to each other,
yet the distance seems to engulf me with despair.
The distance is not real,
but that our souls are on different planes.

I can only look from the pit of my despair,
and need you as you walk on some higher plane.
Though my need for you is warmth,
my want for you brings only cold.

Enveloped by this darkness,
I lay on the cold slab of my consciousness.
Wanting for the absolution of your love.
Wanting for the dedication of my love for you.

I tell you of sorrow if I had not been there for you.
But I do not know if your responses are an admonition,
or if they are words of forgiveness.
For some things can't be forgiven.

I want to put my lips against you,
and pleasure you with words and ways.
Because you are divinity to me.
The heaven on this earth.

I want to spend hours divining the secrets of your Self.
To hear your heartbeat,
To smell the sweet scent of your hair and skin.
To worship what is truly worth all of man's grace.

To Lie Beside You

To lie beside you,
To feel your soft skin,
The curve of hip, waist, belly, and breast.

The rise and fall as you slumber,
Your sweet scent,
Your beauty.

To my Ex

We were fiery and passionate, consumed with the heat of our love.
But that conflagration that burned so bright would burn itself out.
And when the winds of dissolution blew away what was left, those ashes.
There was not else left but the scorch marks on my soul.
That last reminder of you, memoried heat.
Permanently etched on the walls of my cavernous heart.

TOGETHER AGAIN

Together again you and I.
Parted lips speak softened sighs.
Bites and scratches and impassioned cries.

Those things in my mind that I profess to want.
You are all and more, that dreams may haunt.
Yet fear of love, my mind may daunt.

Scent and skin and sound may tell,
Of this vessel dipped in well,
Of our kiss and touch as we fell.

Where with guided hand you were led.
And lowered gently upon the bed.
A friend at times, now a lover instead.

Our first minutes of loves embrace,
Grasps and pinches till the end of the race.
Twice you win with a goddess's face.

Time we spend with taunt and tale,
We have seen pain and joy and wedding bells.
We have heard truth and lie and what is behind passions' veil.

Slowly I kiss neck and shoulder and rest my lips upon your spine.
Bodies in rhythm sound in rhyme.
Ending this night together with one more time.

Now you are gone, yes you must go.
Time together runs so fast and apart so slow.
Yet what there is between us only you and I will know.

Now time ticks by slow and alone.
Music echoes in this lonely home.
As I bleed onto my companioned tome.

Possess you I cannot but I will love you all the same.
As you leave for whence you came.
And this lover's night the dawn shall tame.

WALK WITH ME.

What dream walks before me.
What gentle rain washes me of all the past.
This lovely woman.
This glorious soul.
This beauty of body and spirit.
How grace has shined upon me with your light.
The shadow of fear has no place to linger,
in the imminence of your love.
Peace is upon me.
Peace is upon us.
Warmth radiates from your heart.
An embrace as soft as a loving thought.
A kiss as a promise.
That gentle countenance that stills my soul.
The best qualities of a woman.
Put your hand in mine,
and walk with me.

We Were The Storm

Crack of thunder.
No lightning to warn its way.
You jump against me.
I ask if you are okay.
You say, "Yes".
Then you say, "It kind of excited me."
I smile and continue to excite you after my own manner.
Another strike from Thor's hammer.
You pull me closer.
As if I could be any closer.
And it starts to rain.
The sound of it over our heads.
Soft background to our breaths and whispers.
It is cool tonight for once.
A blessing in the lateness of summer.

What contrast against our dry heat.
Rising from the furnace of our passion.
The thunder breaks like waves against our shores.
Your body rises to meet me.
Craving every inch of contact.
I kiss every inch of you as if this was the last and only time.
Rapture.
The world does not exist outside our cocoon.
Rain and wind cradles our existence.
Time has no meaning.
No laws of God and man exist.
Not for this instance, this moment.
This is ours alone.
A gift that cannot be matched.
A possession no being can steal from us.
You and I are as one.
We will never be closer than as we are at this moment.
You are beauty.
Heaven upon earth.

You are dear to me.
In this briefness of time, you are everything to me.

As fire and earth we mingle.
Arcing those flames that heat us and envelope us as an aura.
Stoking our inferno with words and ways.
And there is distant thunder.
And the rain over our heads.
But the heavens cannot quench us.
Only we each other.
Then the flames burn brightest,
The flames leap high.
Lightning seems to flicker from each touch.
Power pulsating as waves upon each other.
And then we slowly burn and fade.
We begin to ebb to smoldering embers.
Our smoke the mingled scent of our love.
The storm shall pass.
The night shall pass.
Memory shall pass.

But one day again,
There will be thunder.
There will be rain.
And though we may be on far and distant shores,
Memory shall lite upon us of that night.
And we will feel the heat through the cool darkness.
We shall remember the thunder and the sound of the rain.
We shall remember the flames.
And we will remember that in our time,
In that exalted moment in time,
That we were the storm.

WHAT BEAUTY

What beauty lies behind those eyes?
To plumb the depths of that sacred soul.
To touch that tender flesh.
To hold that love against me.
To be together as one.

WHAT IS LOVE

What is love?
How to define it?
Possessive?
No.
Once it was so, I was hers and she was mine.
We said forever, but forever came to end and much sooner than expected,
a harsh and accepted lesson.
What is love?
Love is no single thing, not least between a man and woman.
For so long I had emptied my heart, cavernous and cold, dark silence that
blinded me and made me deaf.
And then a bright and blinding light showed through the darkness.
I shielded my eyes from it, unsure of its source.
What great beauty, its light so warm and soothing.
She came to me and read me a story from her book.
She left those pages in my hands as she went away, her light receding into
the abyss.
I was alone again in my darkness.
Yet I felt those textured pages against my skin, realizing that in my dark
chamber their soft glow remained.
I bound them and put them in their place.
With their light I could see to move within the confines of this small
illuminated sphere.
Yet still in shadows I lay.

Occasions would come when again we would meet, we would read from those pages and renew their light.

Though she was not there she knew that her, our, stories would remain.

Others came and went with stories long and sweet, stories short and passionate, some little more than footnotes of history.

Yet those myriad volumes lit my dark cell, though I realized that my heart was far more expansive than I had hoped.

I still could not discern either ceiling or walls.

Would this void, could this void, ever be filled with that fantastic light?

I sat with the cold stone of my consciousness as my seat facing that warm glow, with darkness behind me.

Oh darkness. I know that 'she' loves me, always with her cold embrace, always wanting me to slide back into her blackness.

She, like death, always accepting and always, like death, never returning. But she whispers to me as any true love does, wanting me, but wanting me to be full and content, even if it is not in her shadowy bosom.

So she shows me that there is not one story, not even one book, for each of my loves, for each woman, but manifold tomes of glorious beauty, friendship, love, lust, companionship, and more.

She led me and showed me, taught me to take one book from its shelf, open it, read its words, feel its beauty, love it, understand it, know this story, this trusted friendship, this amazing woman.

She showed me how to put away that volume and take down another, this one a story of passionate love.

She showed me what I had realized but never truly understood.

That each woman is a countless number of untold tales, and that I could read these stories, some simple, some complex, and that I could read of a woman's love and her friendship, and her hardship, in their turns.

If she wanted companionship, that is what we picked from the varied array.

If she wanted a lovers embrace, that is what we would pick.

What use in carrying these stories by the exhausting armload?

It is so much better to enjoy them one at a time, savoring every word, every nuanced line, fingers tracing the structured elements, the flow of whispered thoughts.

Friend? Lover? Any and all of these things.

Selected as needed and stored in their honored place until the desire to revisit them is at hand.

This glorious way to savor the delicious complexity of a woman.

That is the key!

How I love them!

Voracious and unquenchable is my desire to look upon their loveliness.

Perhaps one day I will see that high ceiling, those farthest walls.

Perhaps there will be a story of such great magnitude that all shall become clear and no shadow will fall upon my heart.

Perhaps.

But for now darkness has her arms draped around my neck, her black tresses falling about my shoulders, her pale cheek against mine.

My constant companion, my love.

And I sit and stare at the golden glow.

That of stories told.

Wondering of what tales the future may hold.

The End.

WILL I EVER KNOW LOVE AGAIN

Will I ever know love again?
Will I ever feel its soft touch?
Feel it reach inside of me?
Feel it draw out the best that is within me?
Or have I met that rough end?
The coarse end of the rope.
Will I ever look again into eyes that truly love me?
And return that immensity to them?
I want to.
With all my heart.
With all that I have.
To give of myself, everything.
But what holds me back?
Fear?
Of what?
Loving someone who does not love me?
Or not loving someone who does love me?
I have tasted the bitterness of both drinks.
The one, I could not make her love me.
My best was never enough.
The other I feared to love,
To spare myself the pain.
But I should have loved her.
Truly and devoutly.
For I lost her with my ambivalence.
And spared myself no pain.
Indeed, all the more for having treated her so ill.
For that I have reserved myself a place in hell.
The hell inside my mind.
Inside my soul.
But I love her now.
Not too little but much too late.
And I still fear that love.
Is my everything enough to warrant it?
Can I love her as she is meant to be loved?

I so want to feel the beauty of her love once again.
The sweetness and purity of it.
The power of it.
Looking into her eyes robs me of reason.
It provokes in me a profound stillness.
I could lie next to her in the night,
As I could lie by her for eternity.
What is heaven but the softness of her skin?
The hue of her eyes.
The sound of her voice, her laugh.
Yet my mind fights against my heart.
So many reasons not to love her.
Yet my heart refuses to yield.
Reason falls to Eros's wounds.
Why did I let our love fall?
Why didn't I fight?
Why didn't I love her as she loved me?
When she loved me.
Perhaps, indeed, this is the end of love for me.
Never to feel the warmth that derives from that depth,
The depths of a woman's soul.
Perhaps my fate is the cold darkness of an absolute and hollow end.
My eyes have been closed to the truth of love too long.
I may die alone.
But God, at least allow me to die with both eyes open.

WOMEN

Women,
I miss you all tonight.
I listen to the wild wind,
And wish for that primal storm.
The humid heat of our embrace.
Beads of sweat falling as rain,
To salt the taste of our skin.
The swell of your breasts against my chest,
My lips.
The softness of your hair as it glides over my rapture.
The sway of your hips,
Rocking against me.
Oh what is this but the beauty of God?
This is the Goddess.
That ancient and primal knowledge,
That divinity lies in the woman.
Only for men to experience through her ways,
And her sex.
The cruel majesty of nature itself.
That heaven resides at that point,
Where I bring her pleasure.
Where her wetted flesh fills my mouth.
Where the strength of my hands,
Coaxes out the art they were truly made for.
To have the pleasures of a woman's body.
To explore that delicate skin in all of its wonder.
To hear her sighs and supplications,
Her ovations to the divine.
To feel her next to me,
In the silence of the night.
Her soft breaths as music to my ears.
You, women, give me this.
All you take,
Is my very soul.

YOUR SPELL IS CAST

I sit in the cool darkness of the auditorium,
A few lights beaming down here and there.
But then I see you,
Lit as by the divine hand of God.
Soft light filtering down on your golden locks.
Like a vision of some Norse Goddess.
Slender pale neck subtly exposed.
Light and shadow play upon the line of your jaw.
The soft rosiness of your cheek.
Slight freckles that must dazzle in the warmth of sunlight.
Pink lips that move with fullness and passion as you read to yourself.
God you are a beautiful woman!
Your hands are feminine perfection.
French manicured tips on nimble fingers.
The way you touch the pages as if they were the face of a lover.
I could watch you forever.
This is heaven to me.
Angelic voice, so soothing.
You turn and look my way.
Gray eyes turning me to stone.
Cool and fierce as the northern sea.
Slightest of smiles you offer me.
Do those keen eyes deduce my form in the darkness?
Or do you feel the adoration of my gaze?
The worship reserved for you in my heart and mind?
You turn back.
Now you smile as you read those words to yourself.
Such an interesting and beautiful habit.
Pulling those words form the page and giving them life and power,
Seemingly with the force of your sweetened breath.
The slight rise and fall of your chest as you speak.
I am fascinated by every tenseness and movement of your body.
Mesmerized by you.
The play of light against your hair,
Shimmering down to your lower back,

Curling over your shoulder and down your slender arms.
Your spell is cast.
My mind forever enslaved to this beautiful moment.
I will never forget you or your beauty,
Though I never knew you.